Depression Finance: How Bonus
Compensation Motivated
America's Financial Crisis

ISBN: 1-4528-8632-6
ISBN-13: 9781452886329

Depression Finance: How Bonus Compensation Motivated America's Financial Crisis[1]

Dr. Michael La Crone

2010

---

1   The first title of this book was "The Depression of 2008: They did it to Us Again". This title was an attempt to metaphorically connect the depression of 1929 to the banking bailout of 2008. Quite rationally, readers interpreted the title as a prediction even though the book was published after 2008. To correct my poor choice of the first title, I considered several other title ideas. The first title idea that most accurately described the book's content was "Depression Finance: How Bonus Compensation of Self-Dealing Corporate Insiders Motivated the Engineering of America's Financial Crisis. The title was too long, so it was trimmed down to the current title. You will also note that the end notes are out of numerical order. Adding two new end notes for this edition made it impossible to keep them ordered.

Dedication

To Chandra Wati for her love and friendship.

To David Ahn for his friendship and for his help to get right the PDF of the graph in this book.

To all the Mom and Pop, and Grandma and Grandpa investors who lost some, much, or most of their stock investment money to the self-dealing deceit and fraud of bankers, stock brokers, and management insiders. This is, of course, a harsh indictment, but it is by no means an exaggeration.

The civil war of 1865 was desperate and deadly, but the outcome for society would be reconstruction as one nation or two nations. One nation based on individual freedom and the other based on freedom for some and slavery for others. As egregious as this outcome would have been, the first and most important revolutionary challenge for America was in 1776. At that time countrymen fought to unchain themselves from predations of a King. The foe was well defined and most of the time obvious. Today the revolutionary challenge comes from the leadership of our corporations and our own government. The foe is stealth and parasitic. Instead of declarations and guns of the King, today we face deception and self-dealing achieved by corporate insiders through the use of financial devices and corrupt deal-making politicians. Just as the King in 1776 would transfer the wealth of our citizens to his own account and continuously burden American citizens by his illegitimate claims, today stock brokers, corporate managers and Wall Street bankers are transferring the wealth of our citizen's retirement savings to their personal accounts by their illegitimate claims. After 30, 40, or even 50 years of hard work and sacrifice for their retirement savings, many American lives reek of financial failure not of their doing, but at the hand of deceptive self-dealing by America's stock brokers, corporate managers, and Wall Street bankers. By stealth use of invisible financial transactions, these insiders have been compensating themselves billions of dollars in shareholders' money.

Through conscious and deliberate behavior, bankers, brokers, and management insiders have lowered the standard of living and degraded the quality of life for millions of people. This paper details the implications of financial insiders using gift and optioned stock to transfer unearned wealth into their personal accounts from the earned wealth of stock market investors.

Self-interest in the absence of coercion or deception implies that a person has the liberty to voluntarily work for the means and ends that satisfy his or her needs and wants. Working under coercion or deception implies that a person is serving the self interest of those using the coercion or deception.

Self-serving implies that a person is in a position of power. That power provides opportunities for a person to improve their personal wealth through the use of that power.

Self-dealing implies that a person is in a position of power. That person uses their power to transfer unearned wealth into their own account from the earned wealth of others.

Introduction

The purpose of this text is to walk the reader through how insiders are gaming stock investors out of their money. The same old deceptions and devices used in 1929 to cheat stock investors are being used today. The game is the same as it was in 1929, only the people and technology have changed.

I explain in the book the reason why executive insiders buy back stocks and make loans that will default. Corporate executives are motivated to buy back stocks which translate into a boost in the company's stock price. Mortgage loan executives are motivated to make bad loans to increase corporate earnings which translate into a higher stock price. A higher stock price translates into maximization of the executive's gift and optioned stock compensation. In the last ten years, bonus compensation in the form of gift stock has transferred over $100 billion into the accounts of executive insiders from money paid-in by stock investors.

Bonus gift stock is a zero-sum gain for insiders and a zero-sum loss for stock investors. I also explain how gift stock compensation is a form of equity skimming that amounts to a Ponzi scheme. Executive bonus stock compensation is nothing less than a greedy wealth transfer from the stock purchase money of widows and orphans, Mom and Pop investors, mutual funds, and 401 K accounts. These self-dealing bonus transactions meet the legal definition of a fraud on the market. No well informed rational person would expose their life's savings to such a scam. The problem is that there is no visible links between stock investors' losses and executive insiders' gains. This is known by regulators who essentially serve as a fig leaf for executive insiders.

When you observe a factory producing output for the market, it is producing units of production. The money paid to employees is represented in earned units of purchasing power. When a person buys a stock, the stock represents a unit of ownership rights derived from earned unit of purchasing power. The value of a person's ownership in a stock represents ownership rights in the company that issued the stock. These ownership rights represent a time value investment in the future growth and earnings of the company. All actions by a company's management to transfer a stockholder's ownership rights of the cash value in a stock to their personal accounts without a unit of compensation for loss are thief of shareholders' purchasing power. Taking gift shares is a pump and dump game. Insiders do what they can to pump up the prices of hundreds of millions shares and then dump them on the market. One technique used to re-inflate the stock price is to buy back the company's stock with company earnings.

It is the responsibility of a company to pay managers in units of earned purchasing power from its earnings, and not from the paid-in capital investment of stockholders through gifts of shareowners money. Gift and optioned shares for executive managers represent a self-dealing zero-sum game. There is no market exchange. Gift and optioned stock are a one sided grant that provides executives a riskless gain when they cash out their free and discounted shares on an unsuspecting and unknowing public. Two of the most egregious examples are Charles Schwab, retired CEO of the Schwab Company and Meg Whitman, past CEO of Ebay. Mr. Schwab took over 10 million gift shares and over $500 million in shareholder money. Meg Whitman took millions of gift shares and over $500 million in shareholder Money. Together they have taken over a billion dollars in shareholder money. They are poster people for insider self-dealing. Like the Mafia in the 1920s and 1930s, who through their bribes of politicians in New York City, which give them freedom to sell drugs; Wall Street insiders have used their bribes of congress (through campaign contributions) to legitimize their skimming of shareholders' money.

According to Caroline Binham in a Bloomberg article (Oct.21, 2009); Brian Grffiths, a Goldman Sachs advisor, speaking in London's St. Paul's Cathedral defended the compensation of Goldman Sachs executives as justified because "inequality helps all". He was quoted as saying "We have to tolerate the inequality as a way to achieve greater prosperity and opportunity for all". The moral to be gained by Mr. Griffith's pronouncement is that not only will a self-dealing sycophant praise as virtuous the corrupt and criminal behavior of his pay master, but he will do it in a house of God. Christians beware, the Devil can preach in the house of the Lord as well as on the floor of the U.S. Congress.

The Depression of 1929

Unresolved questions linger concerning what caused the Great Depression of 1929. Speculative opinions about the crises were rampant in the 1930s. Some say it was caused by the Federal Reserve mismanagement of interest rates and the mismanagement of the money supply. Interest rates were set too high and the money supply was not adequate to stimulate the economy's recovery from an otherwise deep recession. Some say that profligate consumer spending helped to bring on the depression. Technology had helped to create many new products like the radio, the car, and passenger flight. Some attribute inventory cycles, European economic activity, and the list goes on…None of these theories account for the wealth, estimated in the billions of dollars, that was transferred from the working class into the personal accounts of bankers, stock brokers and corporate managers.

The depression was investigated by Congress, academics, and the media, none of them went to the source of the problem to discover the root cause. They all discovered and extensively analyzed symptoms associated with the depression, but none uncovered the depression's origin. Some economists suggest that Federal Reserve's policies led to the depression. Reacting to stock market losses that reduced liquidity, investors withdrew their savings from banks. As panic set in, a lack of confidence in the financial system led to a run on the banks. Banks that could not meet liquidity demands failed. Lack of confidence in the dollar, backed by gold, the Federal Reserve increased interest rates and reduced the money supply causing a recession to become a depression.

Andrew B. Able and Ben S. Bernanke[1], current Chairman of the Federal Reserve, discussing events associate with recessions, make reference to selective economic data that supports an economic cycle theory of the Great Depression. An economic cycle is caused by many events taking place in an industrial economy. Oil supply shocks, war, technological changes, etc…One or a combination of these evens turns an economy at its peck into a downward trend. The downward trend feeds on itself until a bottom is reached, and then a new cycle begins. Able and Bernanke omit some important considerations of what was the driving cause behind the bank failures and what caused shareholders' wealth to be transferred into the personal bank accounts of bankers, brokers, and corporate management insiders. The stock price bubble that finally burst was filled with manipulations by stock market devices, deceptions, and frauds created by Wall Street insiders for the purpose of cashing in their gift and optioned shares at the highest price that they could drum up. Able and Bernanke's reasoning allows for the process of more stock price bubbles driven by the same devices, deceptions, and frauds. Their solution is to bailout the banks destroyed by corrupt insider behavior, but leave the felons their ill gotten booty.

According to the authors, Gary B. Nash, Julie Roy Jeffrey[2]:

The stock market crash was more symptom than cause of the economic collapse. Weak banking systems in both Europe and America, the rise of protectionism, the drop in farm prices, and the decline of purchasing power all foreshadowed the economic disaster that would follow the stock market debacle.

These authors have confused original cause-and-effect relationships with the economic and institutional consequences. The Great Depression was the result a huge wealth transfer from Main Street savings to Wall Street bank accounts. How the pockets of Wall Street bankers and corporate managers' were filled with shareholders' money is a direct cause-and-effect relationship.

According to K. Fred Skousen "The aggregate value of all stocks listed on the New York Stock Exchange was $89 billion before the market decline in autumn of 1929." In 1932, the aggregate value of stocks was only $15 billion—a drop of $74 billion from 1929."[1] Where did that $74 billion go? It went into the pockets of stock manipulators like Joe Kennedy the father of assassinated president John F. Kennedy. As we will see later, $74 billion was a lot of money to lose from of Mom and Pop savings.

As explained in a report to the House of Representatives, stock investor losses in 1929 were implicitly caused by the corrupt self-dealing of stock brokers and Wall Street underwriters:

During the post-war decade some 50 billions (sic) of new securities were floated in the United States. Fully half or $25,000,000,000 worth of securities floated during this period have been proved to be worthless. These cold figures spell tragedy in the lives of thousands of individuals who invested their life savings, accumulated after several years of effort, in these worthless securities. The flotation of such a mass of essentially fraudulent securities was made possible because of the complete abandonment by many underwriters and dealers in securities of those standards of fair, honest, and prudent dealing that should be basic to the encouragement of investment in any enterprise. Alluring promises of easy wealth were freely made with little or no attempt to bring to the investor's attention those facts essential to estimating the worth of any security. High-pressure salesmanship rather than careful counsel was the rule in this most dangerous of enterprises

Equally significant with these countless individual tragedies is the wastage that this irresponsible selling of securities has caused to industry.[2]

The scenario in the following short vignette will help to simplify the logic of a stock market scam by linking the relationship of direct cause-and-effect, and resulting consequences. Cause-and-effect defines a problem and its consequences are the manifestation of symptoms that many analysts attribute as cause. Symptoms of the financial crisis took on a life of their own creating new cause-and-effect relationships:

Suppose three con men, (circa early 1900s) from the east, enter a small town in the west with a plan to swindle the population out of their life's savings. They had conspired with the corporation's management and some Wall Street bankers to act as legitimate stock dealers to represent an eastern company to sell ownership shares. No one would know that they and the others were in business for themselves.

This was a prototype swindle, which if successful, could be accomplished in other small prosperous towns. The con men's plan was to get as much money out of the town's people as they can get and then get out fast. They would wire the money to bank accounts set up for their purpose and no one would ever know where the money went. They had the seed money needed to start-up a stock brokerage and a printing press to produce elegantly styled stock certificates.

Soon they went to work making friends and persuading the town's people to buy stock in a big eastern corporation. They talked about their many connections to Wall Street wealth and Washington's political elite. Before long they convinced a few of the town's people to invest. Next, the con men snowballed the stock price. That is, they artificially increase the stock price. The first share sold for $1. Two weeks later, shares are selling for $10, and a month later, shares are selling for $50. They would tell shareholders that company's earning went up causing the stock price to rise. Investors didn't know that earnings of the eastern company had no connection to the phony price increases of shares they bought. The con men would pay the early investors with money received from new investors.

The few people, who were growing wealthy, thought of themselves as very smart investors, and were soon sharing the secret of their great fortune with the whole town. Shortly, the stockbroker office was crowded with people wanting to become new investors. The con men would work all night printing up new shares to be exchanged for the people's savings. Some enthusiastic investors even borrowed money to buy shares. When the con men calculated that they had sold all the shares they could, they loaded up their wagon in the middle of the night and quietly drive out of town.

Now that the knife has been buried deep in the back of stock investors, there is a twist of the blade. The town's sheriff and his deputy trailed these con men back to the eastern city where the company was located. The sheriff decided to talk with the company's president and board members hoping to get a lead on where to find the criminals that robbed his town. He could not believe his ears when told by the president that those men were employed by the company. The president explained that the board had awarded themselves and the president gifts of bonus stock as a way to align their interests with shareholders. At the time shares were sold in the west, their price was high. However, the price has since dropped to a penny a share. The president told the sheriff that the town's shareholders could come to the company and they would be paid the going market price. There was nothing the sheriff could do. The president explained that they had sold their gift stock in many small towns over the past few months. He told them that Congress had made legal the practice of allowing managers to award themselves gift and optioned stock and then sell these shares to investors.

How did the share price drop to a penny? The town's people put the money in that drove the stock's price up, and the company's executives took the money out that drove the stock's price down. Today, hundreds of millions of "bonus gift" shares are being cashed out by brokers, bankers and company executives. These insiders are not worried because they know that the law is on their side and that there will always be new investors waiting and wanting to get a bargain price on the share of a growing company. How did "bonus gift" stock become legal? The enormous "gift stock" bonus awards given by corporate boards to themselves for their personal accounts at first appear to be legitimate because these gifts have been legalized by Congress, however, the legal status of gift stock was conceived and legitimized on fraudulent premises and deceptive principals.

Wall Street bankers, stock brokers, and corporate managers lobbied Congress, and gave congressional finance committee members huge campaign contributions. For those investment bank insides with money, this is a stealth and persuasive approach to self-dealing for financial gain through buying political patronage.

The con men's acts were cause, the impoverishment of the town's people was effect, and everything after that was consequence. People desperate for cash made a run on the bank; people could not purchase the volume of goods and services that they were buying and had to make do with their savings left in the bank. The town's mayor, wanting to bring some cash back into the bank, created a special tax that was loaned to the bank to be used for loans to credit worthy customers. This did nothing for those who, after years of work and sacrifice, were impoverished and penniless. As some citizens, for lack of money, began to beg in the streets, the mayor created a new tax to provide them with some financial support. People, burdened by high taxes, soon began to move away and over time there was nothing but a ghost town.

Bankruptcies, losses of purchasing power, bank runs, rising unemployment, flight to gold, were all symptoms of the con men's rip-off. The events of 1929 and 2008 were symptoms of a catastrophic direct cause to effect relationship. Like deaths from a parasitic plague brought on by the infestation of blood sucking fleas, losses of purchasing power resulting from the stock market crash were consequences.

Robert L. Heilbroner[3] provides an excellent survey of preceding and concurrent economic conditions leading up to, and during the depression, as well as consequential conditions emerging from the depression. Preceding the depression, corporate leaders, compensating themselves in stocks, were using pyramid schemes to create monopolistic control over multiple corporate entities while bankers, compensating themselves in stock, were lending money on margin to promote the purchase of stocks. Concurrently, there were financial pressures on sectors of the economy brought about by technological innovations. Small volume farm incomes were declining as a result of competition with newly mechanized farms. Mechanized farms used economies of scale to reduce competitive market prices below the cost of production for small volume farms.

Some conditions can be linked as a consequence of strategies by corporate leaders. Heilbroner details how productivity gains were derived from the advances in new technology. At the same time wages for labor were declining; instead of sharing productivity gains with labor, corporate managers were adding gains to bottom line profits. This is exactly what is occurring in today's market. Reports of a stock market recovery based on corporate earnings are all over the new. Likewise, reports of a jobless recovery are being reported. The connection is that managements are showing profits, but not using the money to increase employment. Their strategy is stock price maximization. Corporate managers, (stock brokers, and Wall Street bankers too) are arbitrage[1] seeking profit maximizers, not fools or altruists, and their profit strategy can easily be seen as a way to boost the company's stock price and the value of

---

1   Gift stock arbitrage is where an insider is able to use free and optioned shares to make a risk free gain between the price paid (nothing or next to nothing) and the price sold the shares (the market price of the stock). The insider sells his gift shares on the open market taking the paid-in capital of outside investors. He is essentially pumping out investor money that supports the stock price.

their bonus stock compensation so they can reap the gains. A parallel of cause and effect can be recognize between the decline of income for labor in 1929 and the decline in value of 401 (K) retirement accounts for labor in 2008. It is the connection within and between cause and effect relationships that link management strategies to company profitability. Likewise, it is the connection within and between cause and effect relationships that link management compensation to shareholders as the money source of management compensation.

Here is what happened to investors in 1929, (as well as 2002, and 2008). This explanation of the depression has not been offered to account for what led to the Great Depression of 1929 (or the depressions of 2002 and 2008).

Billions of dollars in savings were transferred out of stock investors' wealth and into the pockets of Wall Street, stock brokers, and corporate management insiders. The year 1929 was at a time when people earned, on average, $6,000[4] a year or about $28 a week and the savings rate was 4.5%[5]. Many stocks sold for $100 and more. Imagine the consequence of a stock investor losing $100 where (savings)/.045= $2,222 in earnings needed to be replenish their $100 in savings-[$2,222x.045=$100]. For the average worker, this would mean $2,222/$28= 79 weeks of earnings, or a year and a half of work just to earn back the $100 lost. Now think about billions of dollars stolen from shareholders who were earning $28 a week. A huge amount of purchasing power was permanently lost.

The argument that a weak banking system, a drop in farm prices, or declines in purchasing power were *causes* of the Great Depression is without merit. These factors were all symptoms manifested as a consequence of a decline in stock investors' wealth. The flaws in banking laws were created by the bankers and for the bankers; income and price declines followed the decline in savings, and were merely subsequent to the underlying loss of wealth which was the real cause.

Many previous accounts for the depression depend upon theoretical associations between banks, institutional Wall Street, and a few powerful Wall Street brokers. They link stockholders' losses to the weaknesses of government efforts at regulating corporate entities. Their metrics are based on summary statistics of corporate earnings, the rhetoric of Wall Street, and the general economic conditions, etc...

In 1929 the economy was growing and bank accounts on Main Street were filling-up with money in the form of savings. Savings were accumulating from the technology revolution and growth in international trade. Wall Street bankers, seeing an opportunity to exchange stock certificates for real money, promised new investors a stake in the growing wealth of new production companies. Some of the old companies were quickly migrating to the new technologies of 1929. The average person working in a shoe store or gas station could become part owner in General Motors, General Electric, Pan American Airlines, and numerous railroad companies.

Public ownership took the form of stock holding. Just as in the vignette, the first investors to buy into a developing stock market boom were growing rich. They were written about in news papers and talked about on the radio. Their stories were inspiring and inviting. The local barber had bought a few shares, not too many, because he wanted just enough to finance his retirement. The stock market had rewarded him with a pile of cash. However, there were no meaningful regulations to protect the interests of stock investors; the depression was just a matter of time.

The seed of this rip-off began when someone on Wall Street came up with an idea that changed the rule governing stock ownership rights. This was an insider's idea that could not be let out to the public. The idea was to reward top bank managers, stock brokers, and corporate managers with bonus stocks. Stocks are a financial substitute for savings accounts. Bonus stocks took the form of stock options. Management insiders could buy the stock for less than the market price and then sell it in a market where stock prices were rising. Outsider stock investors didn't know then and most do not know today who pays for these bonus stocks. The money taken out of the stock comes from outside investors. The price is paid by Mom and Pop investors when the stock is cashed on the market. It is called a zero-sum arbitrage play where the insiders buys the stock for less than market value, and then sell it on the market at the higher price taking a free and riskless gain. Stock option price discounts and gift stocks are a dead weight loss to at-the-money investors. At-the-Money investors are the most recent investors who bought stocks at top of the market prices.

As events evolved, Wall Street bankers and corporate managers were getting rich on these transactions. Then another idea was formulated. How could these insiders speed up the wealth transfer process? The answer was simple, issue *gift shares* so there would be no need for a payment to get the shares and cash them out. Gift shares are the equivalent of counterfeit currency at whatever price the share sells for on the market. The corporations' board would issue gift shares to managers and, of course, to themselves. This is stealth self-dealing.

The wealth of insiders continued to grow at the expense of shareholders. The final phase of this monumental deception and rip-off of Mom and Pop's savings was achieved by the drive to boost stock ownership and thus stock prices through a national marketing effort. Wall Street bankers hired stock touts who peddled stock as far away as San Francisco by hyping the anecdotal success of a few outsiders. Stock touts were out to weasel Grandma and Grandpa, widows and orphans' charity funds, children's' piggybanks, anyone with savings, out of every savings dollar for the purchase of stocks.

Bankers were busy printing more and more free shares for themselves knowing that a collapse was inevitable. The bankers would stay silent. Quietly, these Wall Street bankers and corporate managers would amass huge fortunes from the retirement savings of young and old, poor and rich (outsiders), who had no knowledge of the underlying scheme.

The Great Depression brought misery to millions of people. Congress held hearings, pointed the finger at a few bankers who had media recognition, passed a few laws that were supposed to regulate stock market abuses, but they never uncovered the real underlying cause of the depression. In 1929, people across the country were bankrupted by their stock market losses. Bankers, stock brokers, and corporate managements' amassed great fortunes giving themselves free and optioned shares of stock. They are doing exactly the same thing today. I have a data set of twenty-five corporate executives from only five companies that have received *over **102** million gift shares*. That means one hundred and two million investors have been or will be cashed out of their stock money. Who will make up for these losses? Management insiders are hoping new investors will reinflate stock prices. In my book, *The Charles Schwab Stock Rip-off*, I present in graphical form how insiders skim shareholders' money and the consequences for At-The-Money investors who are the first to lose.

The depression of 2008 was a reenactment of 1929, and until now, Wall Street bankers, stock brokers, and corporate insiders have escaped justice for the same crimes committed against Mom and Pop investors in 1929. According to Frederic S. Mishkin[6] the worst deterioration of consumers' financial wealth occurred between 1929 and 1933. Mishkin reports that consumers lost $692 billion (in 1996 dollars), and consumption dropped by over $100 billion. If you take $692billion/.045=$1.54 trillion in earnings needed to regain lost savings.

How is it different this time? There is not much difference in the technique, except for the viral nature of the internet and the sophistication of deceptive dealings. Alan Greenspan pumped up the stock market and the economy into a price bubble with the help of Wall Street expertise. The result was a monumental success for Wall Street insiders like Hank Greenberg from AIG, and Henry Paulson from Goldman Sachs who had a party helping themselves and other Wall Street insiders transform a huge chunk American's saving into bonus money for their personal accounts. Between the years 2001 and 2008, estimates suggest that over $2 trillion dollars has been swept into the private accounts of Wall Street bankers, stock brokers, corporate managers, not including the special stock deals given to international financial insiders in countries like Israel and Saudi Arabia from Mom and Pop investors, 401 (k) accounts, and mutual funds.

According to Erik Banks: "With $6 trillion of market value sucked out of investors' pockets from 2000 to 2003 (maybe half of that from Moms and Pops), lots of those who got burned are in a fighting mood."[7] CNNMoney.com reports that $1.2 trillion one day loss in stock market value was recorded on Sept. 28th 2008.[8] The San Jose Mercury reports that "American households lost $1.33 trillion of their wealth in the first three months of the year as the recession took a bite out of stock portfolios and dragged down home prices."[9] It is difficult to get an accurate number because Wall Street managers, stock brokers and corporate managers do not want public exposure to a shareholders' accounting of their compensation gains. With Congress too busy counting up next year's campaign contributions, the public is not likely get an accounting very soon. How much will Mom and Pop have to earn in order to restore their lost savings of $2 trillion? With a 3% savings rate they would have to earn $2,000,000,000/.03=$66,666,66 6,667 trillion to earn back the $2 trillion of saving losses. Of course the money taken by insiders between 1999 and 2009 could sum to more than $2 trillion. Much of the reductions in purchasing power caused by stock portfolio losses are offset by mortgage loans, other forms of debt, and a return to work till death. It's a win-win game where, using the pretext of aligning management and shareholders' interest through stock compensation, bankers can loot stock investment money and use their banks to loan it back with interest to the shareholders who earned it. If you still have a jot of doubt, read about the billions of dollars, all stockholders' money, ripped-off by insiders like Charles Schwab the CEO $951 million, Gary Winnick CEO Global Crossing $951 million, Phil Anschutz Director QWEST $1.57 billion to name just three on a list of twenty-five between 1999 and 2002 in the article by Mark Gimein "You Bought They Sold" in Fortune 2002. [10]

Many of these stock brokers and management insiders were multimillionaires before their stock rip-off, but their lives are now way better being billionaires. The years of hard work and sacrifice of the beautician, the cop, the pilot, and the teacher, all wiped out by the slick dealing of financial parasites (more on this later).For many people, the lost of their stock market money needed to support a retirement income will be paid in hardship.

In the case of equity stock compensation, the management insiders' gain does not translate into shareholders' gain. Through the use of stock options, insiders are essentially buying $100 bills for $10, $20, or $30. Using gift shares, these insiders are taking $100 bills free. All this money comes out of stockholders' investment funds. Investors didn't need to buy a company's stock; they could merely make out a check to manager's bonuses for $30,000 or $40,000 and sent it to the company. This would save the investor a stock purchase transaction fee and managers wouldn't have to waste their precious time cashing out stocks.

According to John Taine[11], past CEO of Merrill Lynch, Bank of America's CEO Kenneth Lewis acquired Merrill Lynch knowing that the executives of Merrill were to receive $3.6 billion in bonuses before the acquisition took place. Lewis has denied that he knew. The important point is to realize that as Merrill Lynch was going bankrupt, its executives were paying themselves billion dollar bonuses. If you invested $40,000 in Merrill stock how many new investors would need to buy Merrill stock to compensate for the $3.6 billion taken out in bonuses by management? Take the bonus of $3,600,000,000/$40.000= 90,000 people. This means that if you are among the 90,000 people who invested in Merrill Lynch; you can only hope that another 90,000 new investors will invest $40,000 to cover the cost of Merrill's management bonuses. Have no doubt; this is an insidious form of slavery economics. If it took 90,000 people one year to save $40,000; then management insiders took 90,000 years of labor. These insiders have a fiduciary duty to protect the financial interest of all shareholders as own-ers of the company. When Insider's use of their authority to abuse their fiduciary duty by transferring shareholders' wealth to their personal accounts; they are unequivocally parasitic and predatory.

Exploring a corporation's culture from the perspec-tive of an immune system, Arie de Geus[12] makes reference to parasitic behavior by corporate personnel. De Geus Says "destructive parasites can…exist anywhere in the corpo-rate host."[13] "They can be…individuals of power." [14]Accord-ing to de Geus "power can be used to manipulate the defi-nition of 'us' in the service of someone else's strategy."[15] If the company is performing in a self-destructive manner, de Geus recommends that "…You should not ask, 'why is the activity in the interest of the corporation?' "You should ask, 'Whose interest is served by this self-destructive act?'"[16]. This behavior is a form of parasitic capitalism, but it could just as easily be a form of parasitic socialism or parasitic communism. Insider self-dealing is an opportunistic act of theft that is not constrained by political ideology or in many cases by regulatory authority. It is effectively controlled by 50 to 100 years in prison at hard labor with no parole.

One question to answer is how does a writer describe these self-dealing insiders? The literature on Wall Street crime does not have an adequate term to describe those who use stealth to cheat stock investors. When describing criminal behavior, Criminal prosecutors use the most ap-propriate words that fit the crime. Someone who commit-tees a murder is a murderer, rape a rapist, a person who molest children a child molester.

These descriptors reflect causative behavior. In this context, I describe as predatory financial parasites, those people from Wall Street, stock brokers, and corporate management who take personal gain out of shareholders' equity through the device of gift stocks and stock options and use the deception of alignment of management/shareholders' interests. They have received free or deeply discounted bonus money without exchanging any value to shareholders and without taking any risk. They are using their insider's position to compete with shareholders for shareholders money.

What is the difference between an attack by a pirate and an attack by a parasite? A pirate operates in the open and is visible to the victim. A parasite operates by stealth and is invisible to the victim. You know when you are being attacked by a pirate, but you don't know when you are being attacked by a parasite. A pirate uses coercion and a parasite uses deception. A pirate attacks from the outside. A parasite attacks from the inside.

Japan's attack on Perl Harbor was a pirate attack. Japan's attack was a war of visible forms—guns and bombs with devastating functions—loss of life and individual capital. The stealth attack by corporate insiders on the savings wealth of America is a parasitic attack. This is a war of devastating function—loss of individual capital savings without a visible form—self-dealing gift stocks. This ruinous war without visible form that destroys an individual's financial life and economic opportunities has no less a destructive impact as that of a war by physical means. Legitimacy of this war on investors' wealth by stealth process will not be resolved through any thoughtful concern of a bought-off (campaign contributions) and paid-off (future employ-ment as a lobbyist for Wall Street) Congress. The resolution to this war will be decided by the carefully considered de-termination of a court or by the will of a rebellious public.

For some readers, employing for what some consid-er inflammatory and derogatory name calling cannot be avoided to please their sense of propriety. There is noth-ing polite about criminal behavior. Trying to put a valid descriptive identity on the people of inquiry, my interest is not to insult or belittle for any reason, but as a clinical attempt to capture the nature of a person who does what these people do. My purpose is to use the most appropri-ate language that describes the essential nature of their character as presented by their behavior.

Recently, an article was posted on a Harvard Law School blog by Martin Lipton, Theodore N. Mirvis, and Jay W. Lorsch[17] critiquing a proposal by Senator Schumer to in-troduce a "Shareholder Bill of Rights Act of 2009." Without a discussion of the details regarding the proposal and the critique, there is within the proposal and the critique so se-rious a flaw as to make both writings critically defective.

Senator Schumer and the other gentlemen write their opinions based on the assumption that the financial inter-ests of shareholders in a company are homogeneous. This is not a valid assumption and any recommendations that apply to a company's shareholders must differentiate their separate financial interests. As I explain below, there are at least four different positions that differentiate shareholders. There are shareholders who are deep-in-the-money, and shareholders who are at-the-money. Then there are share-holders referred to as in-the-money who are in between shareholders are deep-in-the-money and at-the-money. Finally, there are shareholders who are out-of-the-money. I discuss conflicts created by gift and option stock compensation for managers and how the different ownership positions for deep-in-the-money shareholders are benefited at the expense of at-the-money shareholders. All of these differentiated ownership concepts will be explained in the following section.

Stock Equity Skimming and the Risk Line

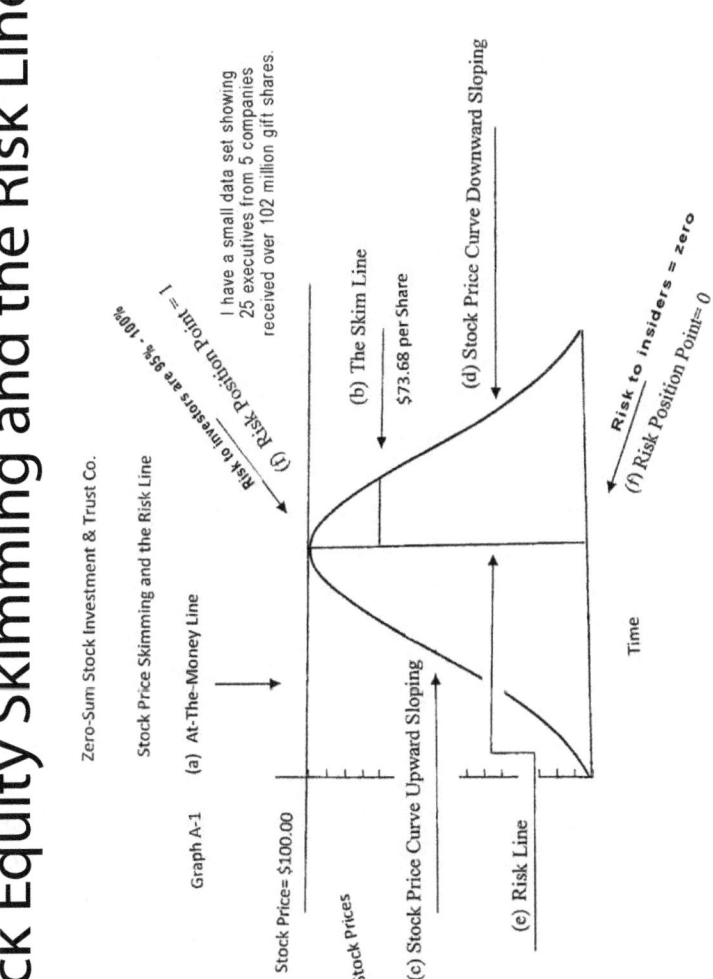

Zero-Sum Stock Investment & Trust Co.

Stock Price Skimming and the Risk Line

Graph A-1   (a) At-The-Money Line

Stock Price= $100.00

Stock Prices

(c) Stock Price Curve Upward Sloping

(e) Risk Line

Risk to Investors are 95% - 100%

(f) Risk Position Point = 1

I have a small data set showing
25 executives from 5 companies
received over 102 million gift shares.

(b) The Skim Line

$73.68 per Share

(d) Stock Price Curve Downward Sloping

Risk to insiders = zero

(f) Risk Position Point= 0

Time

The purpose of Graph A-1 is to introduce you to curves and lines that are used to interpret the various relationships between stockholders and stock equity skimming by executive management insiders. Stock prices are on the vertical axes and time on the horizontal axes.

(a)   The "Stockholders' At-The-Money" line shows the price paid ($100.00) for a share of stock in this company by 401 (k) investors, mutual fund investors, and Mom and Pop investors. If the stock price goes up 2 cents, you are in-the-money by 2 cents, if it drops by 2 cents; you are out-of-the-money by 2 cents.

(b)   The Skim line, just below the at-the-money line, describes how the stock price drops as a consequence of gift and optioned shares sold. It indicates on the risk line how much the stock price declines as a result of insider sales. As shown on the graph, the stock price dropped from $100 per share 26.3 percent to $73.68 per share. Bordered by the risk line, the area from top the stock price curve down to the skim line describes equity losses by outside shareholders that are a result of stealth self-dealing use of asymmetric information[2] by executive insiders. This area represents the invisible hand of executive insiders burglarizing the wallets of outside investors. The only way for investors to regain their losses is through new investors—which is by definition a ponzi scheme. .

---

2   Asymmetric information is knowledge of deceptive conditions used by insiders to exploit outsiders. There is an absence of critical information that would change the investor's evaluation of the investment.

(c)   The upward sloping left side of the bell shaped curve portrays a stock price curve that indicates a share price from zero to $100.

(d)   The downward sloping right side of the bell shaped curve portrays the effect of stock price skimming on a share's price.

(e)   The line bisecting the bell curve is the risk line. It is termed a line instead of a curve because it is beyond the scope of this work to investigate the dynamic influences of stock buybacks and interest rates that may create elastic moves which would turn the line into a curve.

(f)   The arrow pointing to the bottom of the risk line defines managements' risk position and the arrow pointing to the top of the risk line indicates shareholders' risk position.

Note to analysts: In a real world case, data can be gathered to find a representative statistical population distribution (normal or skewed), with the known volume of total shares sold and the volume of shares sold by insiders at a given price. This should provide enough information to estimate the mean; develop a Z score and standard deviations on the risk line. This information could be used to measure expected probabilities of rick for investors given insider sales volume at various stock prices. Of course, a thorough analysis would require results based on several observations under various conditions to enhance reliability and separate correlation from causation. The results of one test would be a rough estimate because exogenous forces such as investor sentiment, stock buybacks, a change in the interest rate, etc…would all have a confounding influence on stability of the statistical results.

First let's define risk!

Risk is defined as a range of probable outcomes extending from zero to one. Zero and one define the point at which risk can no longer be measured because at zero there is no risk and at one an outcome is absolutely certain. As explained above, the line on the graph that drops perpendicular from the top of the stock price curve to the bottom of the graph is the risk line for stock equity skimming. The risk line could be used for any form of equity asset to separate different levels of ownership risk. The arrow indicates that those positioned at the top of the risk line, At-the-Money (ATM) stock investors, are situated at one. This means that they have no risk because their exposure to the real loss of their at-the-money equity is absolutely certain. There is an exception to this conclusion. As I noted in my article, Washington's Bailout of Wall Street; A Rip-off for Investors as well as Taxpayers (of 12-18-2008):

When insiders cash out their free shares, they reduce the total value of the stock outstanding by the amount they took out of the market. If there are many new buyers in the market, the loss will be offset and the price will not go down, but as more free (or optioned) shares are cashed out, less new money will be available to maintain the shares' price and the effects of price skimming will drive the stocks' price down.

Those who are positioned at the bottom of the risk line have zero exposure to equity skimming and therefore have zero risk of loss. This means that insiders receiving gift and optioned stock are receiving riskless unearned free money from shareholders' wealth and that not a dime was paid out by the corporation.

How does it work? Suppose a manager receives one gift share for $100. If he cashes it out on the market, the money is siphon out of the stock. If he holds the share, he is at the bottom of the line in a costless and riskless position. He has successfully transferred ownership wealth from investors at the top of the curve to his personal account as money gain or ownership as a free-loading stockholder. The same device and deceit was employed in 1929 by bankers, stock brokers, and management insiders to divest shareholders of their ownership equity.

There is a self-dealing zero-sum game being played between executive management and investors. Stock investors lose in a mirror inverse relationship what insiders gain. Charles Schwab, the CEO, took over a billion dollars from investors equity by cashing out millions of gift shares not merely from direct investors in the Schwab Company, but through mutual funds and 401 (K) funds. So too did the CEOs and Directors of Goldman Sachs, Global Crossing, JDS Uniphase, Qualcomm, Broadcom, eBAY, The Gap, Microsoft, FedEx, UPS, and many other companies. These insiders are not stock investors; they simply strip out the paid-in capital of investors. Sometimes an executive will purchase five or ten thousand shares to create the illusion that he is an investor, but if you go back far enough, you will find that he has cashed out four or five hundred thousand gift or optioned shares. This is like the bank robber using his stolen loot to open a savings account.

One share of gift stock is theft by fraud. Their fraudulent gains must be returned to those people who earned the money and were defrauded—all of it. You might get the impression that these people are too wealthy and politically powerful to challenge, but if Hitler and his criminal empire could be brought to justice, so too can the financial crimes of these people. If financial justice does not prevail, then democracy in America as we know it is doomed. Political pundits are focused on creating jobs as a way to build an economic recovery, so too was the focus of slave economies.

The risk line absolutely and unequivocally destroys any pretense for the argument that companies who give executive insiders gift and optioned stock create an alignment of interest with shareholders. You buy and own a share at $100 while the executive management insider receives the same share at a cost of zero. When he cashes out that share, he is cashing out your $100 ownership. Because there is ten thousand more investors buying and selling at $100 does not change the essential nature of your loss, it merely confounds the smooth calculation of loss. Why are stock investors equity pools shrinking? Stock investors are not buying corporate cash flows; they are buying executive bonus expenses.

Embedded in the risk line are all the incentives, disincentives, and asymmetric information for buying and for holding a share of stock. At-the-Money investors who lack information on the skimming process are not informed well enough to make sound financial decisions about the exposure of their equity to skimming losses and the illusions touted by stock brokers about the potential rewards. On the other hand, management insiders are well informed of Mom and Pop's retirement equity money is being skimmed for their equity gains from gift and optioned stock with zero risk exposure.

Since stocks are created from money, they are a form of money. Gift and optioned stock is a form of counterfeit money created by insiders for insiders from outsiders' money. Other than pure speculation, the only justification for stock ownership is dividend income. Like all investments, equity principle demands a return on investment and a dividend is the investment return. A stock that does not pay dividends in an environment of stock equity skimming is a pure fraud on stock investors. A stock that gives a dividend in an environment of stock equity skimming is a pure fraud which steals the stockholder's money while providing an enticement.

In a stock market fraught with executive insiders self-dealing where $ 100s of billions are being skimmed; those investors at the top of the curve are at the 90 to 100 percent risk level. This is not rational risk taking. How can this irrational behavior be so pervasive? The answer is twofold. First, there is little or no concern by Congress or Regulators for investors' risk of loss from insider self dealing stock trades. Second, stocks touts make money by pumping up the irrational expectations of naive investors for an irrational investment in stocks. They are the present day snake oil sales people. Charles Schwab and George Gilder are the first two people that come to mind as stock touts. Of course the book shelves are full of half witted bla-bla on the virtues of stocks as an investment. Many of these authors tie partial facts, omissions, and distorted speculations to half truths and lies.

Henry Paulson, former CEO of Goldman Sachs and the treasury secretary to presidents Bush and Obama, wrote a book recently explaining how he saved the nation from financial disaster by initiating his tax payer bailout of the banks. What he omits to mention is the $250 million he took in stockholders' equity as gift stock bonuses for his personal account. How did all that $250 million 401(K) and mutual fund money find its way into Mr. Paulson's pocket?? He doesn't explain how bailing out AIG saved the bonuses of his friends at Goldman Sachs. What Paulson fails to explain is how banking executives used every means possible to drive their bank's stock price up so that they could maximize their personal gift and optioned stock gain. Did they sell mortgage loans that they knew would default? Did they use Collateralized Debt Obligations (CDOs) to boost their bank's stock price? You, the reader, make the decision, but know that their bank's stock price went up, and the executives cashed out $billions.

This same perverse incentive applies to stock brokers and corporate executives who drive up their company's stock price by any means possible. Paulson goes on to explain how a new form of regulation would prevent another financial crises. He doesn't consider the facts that the current regulatory powers which failed to prevent this financial crisis were created in 1933 for the purpose of preventing another financial crisis like the 1929 great depression. There is no reason to believe that any form of regulation can prevent other financial crises as long as Wall Street bankers can use deception and stealth financial devices to indulge in stealing investors' equity through self-dealing. The regulators have been captured by Wall Street. The regulators come from Wall Street and serve the interest of their cohorts on Wall Street. Members of the financial committees in Congress have served as well paid handmaids to Wall Street's executive managers. Does it make any difference that bankers are taking less in bonus stock than they did before? Bailing out banks does not mitigate the financial fraud on investors.

There is a solution to these types of financial crises. The solution is to establish stockowners' equity rights in the same way that homeowners have home ownership rights. The same homeownership money used to buy stocks and that was then stolen out of stocks could not have been stolen out of the home's ownership equity. It was the transfer of money from Mom and Pop's home to stocks that allowed these thieves to divest the equity interest of Mom and Pop. This was not a market loss such as a home's value declining or a stock market loss because outside investors retreated from the market; this was insiders draining the equity pool by giving themselves gift and optioned stock that had no value but for the value paid in by outside investors. There are many ways to cheat stock investors out of their money. If Congress wants to get serious about protecting the stockholder public, it should start by protecting their stockholders' equity rights from the self-dealing interest of those who are in a position to exploit any weaknesses associated with paid-in equity ownership rights.

To summarize, stock equity skimming is a process of converting public ownership capital into insiders' private accounts through the stealth use of device and deceit. This is a transaction where there is no exchange of value for value with shareholders, and the billions of dollars in corporate ownership capital paid for by shareholders is converted to the personal accounts of executive management insiders. Insiders receive a completely costless and riskless wealth transfer. Who says there are no free lunches? Here is an example of millions of free lunches for several generations of management progeny paid for through the investment accounts of widows and orphans and through the life savings of Mom and Pop retirement accounts.

It is not an overstatement to say that bankers, stock brokers, and corporate executive managers are committing a crime against humanity in a stealth war against America's earned wealth. Congress and regulators have done nothing to uncover the real crimes and criminals; instead they prefer to attack abstract entities such as "banks" as irresponsible, "derivatives" as too risky, deficient regulations of trading techniques, and any other excuse that diverts attention away from the people responsible for causing the financial crisis. If you find out who has your money in their pockets, you have found out who stole your money.

The next section on buybacks covers some of the same details found in this section, but with a little more scope. For a more complete presentation of the stock equity skimming process refer to my other book The Charles Schwab Stock Rip-off. In it you will find graph #1 which illustrates the relationship between at-the-money investors' stock price and insiders' gift and optioned stock skimming. To show that when insiders cash out their gift stocks for a gain at stockholders expense, graph # 2 illustrates the zero-sum game between management and shareholders. And, based on information from a Sept. 2nd 2002 article in Fortune, the last graph presents a picture of how Mom and Pop investors lost almost a billion dollars of their stock equity through gift and optioned stock to Mr. Schwab and his executive management team.

Buybacks

Between 1999 and 2008, Standard and Poor's reports that corporate managers in the Standard and Poor's 500 Index have spent over 2.58 trillion dollars buying back their stock[18]. Stock buybacks increase the stock's market price by reducing the number of shares per dollar of earnings. Buybacks are justified by the rationale that shareholders will benefit from the higher stock price. Most of this buyback activity was necessary to soak up the gift and optioned stock cashed out by insiders. Omitted are considerations of the shareholders who will benefit most, those shareholders who will benefit least, and why some will benefit more than others.

There are different risks for shareholders in a company depending on how close the investor's price position is to the market price. For the purpose of illustration, there are four distinct categories of shareholders that can be identified owning the same stock at the same time. They are deep-in-the-money, in-the-money, at-the-money, and out-of-the-money (don't fall *asleep, I'll explain below). These investors can all be at odds with each other over the stock's price for different reasons. The most important conflict considered here is between deep-in-the-money and at-the-money investors. Deep-in-the-money investors have the least risk of loss to their wealth while at-the-money investors have the most risk of loss. Deep-in-the-money investors risk losing gains on their stock price appreciation, but have little risk of losing their initial investment. At-the-money investors have the greatest risk of losing their initial investment. Given that Insiders paid nothing for their gift shares, they are as **deep-in-the-money** as you can get. Let's look at a stock with a market price of $100. If a manager is given 1000 shares, his position is $100 x 1,000 =$100,000. Next, there is the shareholder who bought the stock ten years ago at $50 a share. She is **in-the-money** by $50 (100-50=50). Then there is the investor who just today bought the stock at $100. Since he bought 1,000 shares, he paid $100,000 for his **at-the-money** position.*

Now suppose that as soon as Mr. At-the-money returned home, his wife tells him that she is pregnant, and that they will need their savings for the new baby. Little do they know that insiders want the money that he just invested! Embedded in the share is the right of insiders to give themselves shareholders money as a way to align their interest with shareholders. As you will see, this is a deception. Insiders have lobbied and bribed Congressional approval (campaign contributions) for the right to pay themselves in free stock. Now suppose the Mr. Management Insider, in order to increase the stock price gain on his portfolio of companies producing war materials decides to cash out his gift shares and donate the proceeds to *his favorite charity Terrorist Organizations of the World United against America. The insider cashes out his 1000 gift shares and since there are not enough people in the market to buy up his shares at $100, the stock price falls. Mr. At-the-Money share price drops 20%. He is now in the last category of shareholder,* **out-of-the-money.**

There are two ways that Out-of-the-Money can get his money back. First, he can hope that some new investors (bigger fool) thinks the stock price is cheap and bids the price up with new money. This scenario smacks of Ponzi.

Second, the company can buy back shares creating the illusion the earnings per share is rising. There is a problem with stock buy backs. The money used by companies to repurchase stock comes from earnings. Dividends are the income paid to shareholders for the investment risk of owning stock. Dividends are like the interest paid on your savings account. These are the same earnings that would be used to pay dividends for widows' pension funds. There is also a trade-off for the company. When earnings are expended for buybacks, other investment opportunities suffer. Stock bonus compensation to management insiders comes at a price to other investment opportunities. The money spent on repurchasing stock could be used to hire more employees, (resulting in higher consumption spending by those who do not lose their savings in the stock market), the money could be used to train employees for new technology jobs, funds could be used for research and development of new products or medicines, and the company could use the buyback money to pay for employee health care.

With gift and optioned bonus stock, at-the-money investors don't buy the company's assets that result in long-term earnings. Instead, they buy the management insider's bonus expense that simply removes the investor's purchase money from the stock. This is similar to paying your gardener through ownership in your house. Instead of giving him cash, you give him an ownership position that allows him to cash out all the appreciation that has built up in your house.

The sports analogy used by some insiders to compare their bonus compensation to that of a baseball player does not hold up to logic. The ball player is paid from the voluntary purchase of a ticket for an afternoon of entertainment. The ticket price is known and voluntarily paid while the management insider is paid without the investors' knowledge that their money is being drained out of the stock by managers' cashing out their bonus gifts. There is no voluntary exchange of value for value, but merely a one sided zero-sum gain for the manager at the investor's expense.

Some in Congress and some government officials would have investors believe that losses were God's will. Investors were being punished for their sins. All those billions in lost savings just vanished up to heaven. They certainly would not tell investors that their friends from Wall Street cashed out billions in bonuses, and sent all that money into their personal accounts. After a mountain of investor money was skimmed from the market, few people are willing to replace the losses with their risk capital, and stock market prices will drop. It all worked out very well for Wall

Street bankers. This same scenario played out in the market crash of 2001. Corporate managers in technology companies were channel stuffing (pushing inventory out the door) and giving their customers free inventory (booking the gifts of inventory as sales) to increase company sales. They were managing their earnings to drive up their stock prices. Earnings manipulations by management insiders amounted to deceitful behavior and theft.

Follow the logic. Wall Street bankers are receiving train loads of gift stock and stock options. When these bankers make subprime mortgage loans, the company's earnings go up. When the company's earnings go up, the stock price goes up. When the stock price goes up, bankers' cash out their gift and optioned stocks. If, in a year or two, the loans begin to default, who cares? The Wall Street bankers got all the money they could get from Mom and Pop Investors.

A financial fraud by Wall Street bankers that accomplished the transfer of over a trillion dollars by rigging the market creates a difficult legal challenge. The legal weight of all that stolen money acts as a thumb on the scale of justice. Shareholders' lawsuits can be thwarted by the mountain of shareholders' cash that was stolen. These thieves can use their free money gains to purchase the best legal defense that money can buy. This situation can only be brought back into balance when the power of government steps in to rebalance the scales. As with the lawyers of bankers, unfortunately, the few people in Congress who could be effective against the criminal behavior of Wall Street bankers have been compromised by Wall Street bankers' money.

A recommendation: There can be no spirit of reconciliation by investors who lost their earned wealth to insiders while these insiders posses the unearned wealth of investors. The fraudulent gains from this stock market swindle must be returned to stockholders personal accounts in dollars not stock. If it means that Wall Street bankers sell their homes and go bankrupt, they need to repay all shareholders' losses with interest.

Obama's Pay Czar

Like the swine flu, it appears that Wall Street bankers and corporation managers are preparing to make another attack on 401 (k) retirements, Mom and Pop stock money, and international stock investors' portfolios. First, banks and corporations are retaining cash to make their earnings per share rise. This is a market signal that the recession has bottomed, and it is time to buy stocks. Next, President Obama's pay czar Ken Feinberg, in consultation with Wall Street insiders, has concluded that companies pay too much out of their cash for compensation. Instead, he wants to substitute their company cash compensation by requiring executives take gift and optioned stock. As though gift and optioned stock are a punishment, remember that Steve Jobs, Apple's CEO, took only one dollar a year in company cash compensation and over $200 million in stock compensation. Just as in the Uncle Remus story where Brer-rabbit, knowing he wouldn't be hurt, plans his escape by telling Brer-fox to "roas" him or hang him, but begs, "Please don't fling me into the brierpatch"; these executives beg "please don't pay me in gift and optioned stocks." Finally, many of these executives who broke their banks are now doing all they can to recapitalize the stock market as a way to repay their government loans. *Guess where the money will come from?* Money fund managers, hoping to regain their stock losses, are also hoping the stock market reliquefies.

Wall Street International

Wall Street has become the financial deal maker for the world. Currently, big money is being made by Wall Street bankers using American's savings to fund Chinese production capacity. As our politician's spend more and more to prop-up the banks that caused our financial crises, these well financed politicians (billions in corporate campaign contributions) are putting us deeper and deeper in debt to the world and especially China. America is becoming a nation without an economic base, and there is a cost to America's standard of living, to the financial returns for our America's labor, and to our economic future. This is not an attack on the great productivity of China or on the benefit of international trade; it is an inquire into the use of America's retirement fund controlled by whom, earned by whom, compensated to whom, for the benefit of whom?—those who earned these funds or those who make use of them!

It is capital that drives production capacity and job creation. Capital is derived from savings, and savings are derived from corporate earnings and Mom and Pop's savings. When production and jobs decline as a result of recessionary economic conditions and when jobs are exported to cheap labor markets; Mom and Pop's economic future suffers. The assumption that many underdeveloped countries like China are growing which may create future job opportunities for America does not mitigate the savings losses and job losses to America's current labor market. Technology is not a differential economic advantage in an age when its secrets have become ubiquitous.

As capital is moved off-shore, and American jobs are lost, will America's middle class shrink to accommodate the production class of underdeveloped countries?

Are these Wall Street bankers collaborating with China at America's competitive economic expense? How far should Wall Street bankers be allowed to link up capital investments in foreign economic production before we find out the consequences to our economic future?

Are Wall Street's self-dealings creating a fragmentation of America labor's competitive position? Foreign investments create an obvious payback for Wall Street bankers, but what is the payback for American labor?

Will America become China's low cost labor market? Where is the balance between growing America's international product markets and Wall Street insiders selling out America to foreign interest for personal gain? Three of the nation's leading writers on the subject of CFO (Chief Financial Officer) management practices say that they are "...now seeing the death of the 'captive' in-house shared services model."[19] They explain that "companies will no longer invest in improving back-office administrative productivity..."[20] "Companies will use out sourcing as a path to greater profitability..."[21] Technology will automate routine tasks connecting to a single (global) platform. With this platform, managers will "employ highly skilled workforces at very low cost"[22] from foreign labor markets of India, China, South America, etc...

There is a sense that corporate executives, stock brokers, and Wall Street bankers are not working for America; they are working for themselves on America's money. Recent evidence [3]supports the view that as long as bankers, stock brokers, and corporate executives can buy government patronage and can be subsidized by the financial support of tax payers, they will continue to corrupt legislation, loot stock investment savings, and bankrupt the livelihoods of Americans.

---

3   The New York Times Business section, Bloomberg.com, and the Wall Street Journal are excellent sources of critical information on Wall Street. Four books provide useful analysis and resource information. I do not always agree with the recommendations of the authors, but their research and analysis offers significant insight into Wall Street insiders' corrupt behavior. EriK Banks, *The Failure of Wall Street: How and Why Wall Street Fails—And What Can Be Done About It.* Palgrave Macmillian (Aug. 26th, 2004). Simon Johnson and James Kwak: *13 Bankers: The Wall Street Takeover and the Next Financial Meltdown.* Pantheon (March, 30th 2010). Arthur Levitt, Jr.: *Take On The Street: What Wall Corporate America Don't Want You to Know.* Vintage (Nov. 11th, 2003), and my other book, *Michael La Crone: The Charles Schwab Stock Rip-Off: How Management Insiders are Looting Stockholders' Money,* (BookSurge Publishing (Nov. 11th, 2006) The current book and the Schwab book are the only source of analysis that explains insider self-dealing as a fundamental cause of stock investors' financial losses.*

Endnotes

1   Andrew B. Able, and Ben S. Bernanke, *Macroeconomics,* fifth edition, (Boston: Pearson, Addison, Wesley, 2005), P.P. 276-307.

2   Gary Nash, and Julie Roy Jeffrey, *The American People: Creating a Nation and a Society,* seventh edition, (New York: Pearson Longman, 2006), p. 786.

3   K. Fred Skousen, *An Introduction To The SEC,* Fifth Edition, (Cincinnati, OH: South-Western Publishers, 1991), P.6

4   The House Committee on Interstate and Foreign Commerce, Federal Supervision of Traffic in Investment Securities in Interstate Commerce, Report No. 85, 73d Cong. 1st Sess. (Washington, D. C.: U.S. Government Printing Office, 1934), p.2. As quoted in K. Fred Skousen, An Introduction to the SEC, p. 7

5   Robert L. Heilbroner, in collaboration with Aaron Singer, The Economic Transformation of America, (New York: Harcourt Brace Jovanovich, Inc., 1977), PP. 174-177

6   Paul Gomme and Peter Rupert, *Per Capita Income Growth and Disparity in the United States*, 1929-2003, (Federal Reserve Bank of Cleveland, August 15 2004), P.1

7   www.ebri.org, *EBRI Datebook on Employee Benefits*, Chapter 9: Personal Savings, UPDATED April, 2009, P.4

8   Frederic S. Mishkin, *The Economics of Money, Banking, and Financial Markets*, seventh edition, (Boston: Pearson, Addison, Wesley, 2004), P.624

9   Erik Banks, *The Failure Of Wall Street: How And Why Wall Street Fails And What Can Be Done About It*, (New York: Palgrave Macmillan, 2004), P. 98

10   Alexandra Twin, *"Stocks Crushed,"* CNNMoney.com, Sept. 29, 2008

11   Jeannine Aversa, *"Americans' Net Worth Falls $1.33 Trillion in Q1,"* San Jose Mercury, June 12th 2009, Section E.

12   Mark Gimein, *"You Bought, They Sold,"* With Reporter Associates, Eric Dash, Lisa Munoz, Jessica Sung, "The Greedy Bunch," Fortune, Sept. 2nd 2002, PP 66-74.

13   Michael J. Moore and Dakin Campbell, *Thain Says He Should Have Furnished Merrill at Ikea*, www.Bloomberg.com, Sept.18th, 2009

14   Arie de Geus, *The Living Company*, (Boston: Harvard Business School Press, 1997), P.P.165-167

15   Ibid. P.165

16   Ibid. P. 166

17   Ibid. P.166

18   Ibid. P. 167

17   The Harvard Law School Forum on Corporate Governance and Financial Regulation, http://blogs.law.harvard.edu/corpgov/2009/05/12

18   Standard and Poor's Press Release, *S&P 500 Stock Buybacks Retreat 66% in Fourth Quarter*: Off 42% in 2008, (New York, March 26,2009), www.marketattributes. standardandpoors.com

19   Stewart Clements, Michael Donnellan, in association with Cedric Read, *CFO Insights: Achieving High Performance Through Finance Business Process Outsourcing, (West Sussex, England: John Wiley & Sons, Ltd, 2004) P.vii*

20   Ibid. P.vii

21   Ibid. P.vii

22   Ibid. P.7

Washington's Bailout of Wall Street:
A Rip-off for Investors as well as Taxpayers

By
Dr. Michael R. La Crone (DBA '96-Finance)
12-18-2008

Most insiders on Wall Street would like to turn the page on the current recession so that they could get back to business. The business they would get back to would be doing what they were doing. Namely, using the same old devices and deceptions they used to help create our current financial problems.

What Congress did with the $700 billion bailout money merely buried the financial frauds of Wall Street under a mountain of cash. What Congress didn't do was get to the bottom of Wall Street's misbehavior and take the guilty to task for their financial felonies. Instead, the guilty were given bailout money to re-capitalize the investment banks that these insiders bankrupted. In addition to the money ripped-off from the stock market; our tax dollars are now paying these same Wall Street insiders to employ Washington lobbyists and financially support members of Congress through campaign contributions.

What did not change was the opportunity to use the same old devices and deceptions to continue their "stock price skimming" of new investors' money. When the CEO of Goldman Sachs, Lloyd Blankfein, declared that he would take a dollar a year in compensation, he omitted to mention that he had already free loaded over a million gift stocks and award of stocks. The bailout money will re-inflate Goldman Sachs stock price, so the amount of money coming from these shares would, no doubt, bring in substantially more money than corporate compensation. All at Shareholders' expense!

The critical element missing in all of the Congressional investigatory activity of Wall Street has been to ask "where did all the money go that caused a need for the bailout?" Treasury Secretary Hank Paulson knows "Who got da money." He got over $200 million of da money while he was the CEO for Goldman Sachs. Executives of these Wall Street firms are loaded up with millions of freeloaded shares.

What is stock price skimming? As I explain in my book, The Charles Schwab Stock Rip Off, stock price skimming occurs when an at-the-money (explained below) investor buys $10,000 worth of stock, and within a fraction of a second a manager, Charles Schwab, Henry Paulson, Lloyd

Blankfein cashes out $5 or $6 million dollars of their gift stock. When insiders cash out their free shares, they reduce the total value of the stock outstanding by the amount they took out of the market. If there are many new buyers in the market, the loss will be offset and the price will not go down, but as more free shares are cashed out, less new money will be available to maintain the shares' price and the effects of price skimming will drive the stocks' price down. Let's say that you buy a stock online for $100, this means you are at-the-money for $100. If the stock price declines by $10, you are out-of-the-money by $10. (Dilution of earnings is not directly relevant to stock price skimming.) The only way that the at-the-money investor can get her money back is through new investors. Stock options and gift stock represent a ponzi fraud embedded in the stock purchased by at-the- money investors.

Essentially, insiders are competing with new investors for new investors' money without putting up any money. There is no risk for insiders and no return for investors. This strategy selectively skims new at-the-money investors' funds and does not affect those investors who are deep-in-the-money (bought stock at a lower price). Over time, at-the-money investors are squeezed out of the stock because total new investors' money has not grown fast enough to offset what has been siphoned off the market. Mr. Schwab has ripped off more than a billion dollars of at-the-money investors funds and, so far, gotten away with it. Oracle CEO Larry Ellison has cashed millions of gift shares. This is money that is not reinvested in the market.

From investment banks such as Goldman Sachs and J. P. Morgan, to Commercial banks, Bank of America, Wells

Fargo, to technology companies, Cisco, Intel, Oracle, to blue chip companies, IBM, Proctor and Gamble, Dell, to oil companies, Exxon, Conoco Phillips, to pharmaceuticals, Pfizer, Merck, the list goes on and on; self dealing management insiders have received millions of free shares that they are cashing out for hundreds of billions of dollars in shareholders' money. Again, this money does not return to the stock market. The companies that gave insider managers these free shares did not pay a cent for them and, besides a tax deduction, get no money for them.

New at-the-money investors do not want to put their savings in to a stock for an opportunity to get their money skimmed by insiders, but Congress has not disclosed this pig-in-the-poke, and that's the way self- dealing insiders on Wall Street like it. What these managers are taking from shareholders is unearned and parasitic. Stock price skimming of shareholders' equity is a vicious fraud on unsuspecting investors brought about by Wall Street's corrupt influence on Washington. Investors lost savings that took many years to save and it will take many years of savings to restore all the purchasing power lost. Young people have 30 years of work ahead of them to recover, but older people will never recover. No government bailout will restore the earned savings stolen by this egregious insider freeloading. Insiders took their gains by committing fraud on investors. If government wants to restore this economy then it needs to require that management insiders return, from their insider accounts, the hundreds of billions of dollars in shareholders' money.

On Money and Water

By
Dr. Michael R. La Crone
May 27 2010

What physical property most accurately compares with money as a way to describe the function of money? Many writers have sought to compare blood with money. Money is the blood of enterprise. Many other writers have sought to compare milk with money. Money is the mother's milk of Wall Street finance. Neither blood nor milk capture functional dimensions of the physical properties that translate into the functional dimensions of abstract money and how it works. The best physical property to compare with money is water. Both money and water have a natural quality that acts more as a catalyst than as a nutrient for cells. Water unlocks the potential of a seed so that it may grow into a lawn, a flower, a vegetable, or a tree. Money, like water, unlocks the potential of an individual so that she or he may intellectually grow into a qualified nurse, engineer, teacher, or doctor. Deprived of water, potential of the seed withers; deprived of money, potential of the individual withers.

There would be no life on earth without water. Neither blood nor milk would exist. It is water that brings life to all living matter. Think about water for a moment. Imagine you have a garden. You have beautiful flowers, fresh vegetables, a green lawn, and some very healthy fruit bearing shade trees. Now imagine that by degrees the water to your garden was cut off. First, the lawn would start to turn brown and die. Next, your flowers and vegetables would start to wither and at last drop. Finally, the trees would stop producing fruit and begin to waste away and die. A seed will wither and crash for lack of water acting as a catalyst to stimulate and sustain its growth.

There would be no savings wealth without money. Think about money for a moment. You want to buy a cup of coffee? You must pay for it with money, assets or your labor. What are you going to do? Trade one of your shoes? Work a half hour at the restaurant so you can have your coffee? Now imagine an economy green with money. Jobs are plentiful. All levels of intellectual capacity have access to employment that pay well for the time and cost to achieve these levels of intellectual skills. A life time of savings earned from a life time of work and sacrifice is well protected in banks and investments by laws against misuse by fiduciary management. Now imagine that the laws failed and by degrees all the money in a major investment began to disappear. Jobs are being lost to layoffs. New jobs are not being created. The savings rate dropped below zero (people are living on borrowed money). A human's potential will wither and crash for lack of money as a catalyst to stimulate and sustain his or her material and intellectual growth.

Now suppose that ten million gardens were deprived of water. Beyond the loss of the gardens, there is loss a comfort provided by the lawns, loss of beauty and fragrance provided by the flowers, loss of food for the table provided by the vegetables, and loss of fresh fruit nutrition provided by the trees. All the labor and money spent to grow the garden lost.

Suppose that ten million people lost much of their money. Beyond the loss of money in savings, there is a loss of individual purchases by a multiplier of tens of thousands. Cars are not purchased, homes are not bought, college educations forgone, surgeries skipped, vacations, appliances, clothes, all made unaffordable by loss of money. And don't forget, tax revenues are not collected on purchases made unaffordable. On a personal level, the father is reduced to a failure in the eyes of family and friends. How could he lose the family's savings? The reality is that he and a million other fathers are the victims of financial parasites who use a trusting relationship and stealth to deceive and loot.

What would the gardeners do to bring their gardens back to life? What would these people do to bring their finances back to life? Gardeners would need to fight in court to restore the supply of water. People would need to fight in court to restore their supply of money. The first question to answer is what happened to the water supply that caused gardens to go dry? People would ask what happened to the money supply in investments that caused people's bank accounts to go dry. Answers to these questions contain their solution.

If the water was diverted to someone else's garden by violating the rights of the gardener to her ownership access, then the law must step in and stop the manipulation. If the money was diverted to someone else's account by violating the rights of the people who earned the money, then the law must step in and stop the manipulation. The loss of ten million gardens is heart breaking; the loss of savings money from ten million investors' accounts is devastating. The water must be restored and the garden must be returned to its original state as before the manipulators abused the gardener's rights. The gardener must be made whole again. The money must be returned to those from whom it was taken and their lives must be restored to their original state as before the manipulators abused the owner's rights. The investor must be made whole again.

In the current financial crises large pools of money have been drained from one sector of the economy into the bank accounts of others. So where did that money go? In whose account will that money be found? If one looks, the money will be found in the personal accounts of fiduciaries such as bankers, stock brokers, and corporate executives whose duty it was to protect the interest of those from whom the money was transferred.

How did all the bankers, stock brokers, and corporate executives transfer the savings wealth produced by investors? They didn't exchange any value to pay these investors! Just like a canal used to siphon water out of a lake, they did it by stealthily giving themselves hundreds of millions in gift stock used as a contrivance to transfer over a hundred billion dollars out of investors' accounts.

They are getting away with this monumental crime because, as insiders, they control the information and because they are taking the money from many people. If someone stole over a hundred billion dollars from a government entity or a corporation, they would have a better than average chance of getting caught. Bernie Madoff only stole fifty billion, but he was eventually caught. What makes this theft so insidious is the close relationship of regulators to the insider thieves. What makes it more invidious is that at times the regulators and potential future politicians are in a position as an insider. Four people represent this point; Henry Paulson, former treasury secretary in the Bush administration and Goldman Sachs CEO, and Mary Schapiro, current Head of the Securities and Commission, and former board member of both Duke Energy and Kraft Foods.

Being well aware of the source money, both of these individuals received gift stock as bonus compensation—Paulson over $500 million and Schapiro tens of $1000s. Two candidates running for political office in California, Meg Whitman, former eBay CEO and Carly Florina, Former Hewlett-Packard CEO were both enriched by bonus gift and optioned stock. Whitman took over $500 million and Florina only $39 million. They are now using this money to fund their political campaigns and buy their way into a government position. All their gains were zero-sum stockholder losses.

Letter to Senator Carl Levin

4-28-2010
Michael Roy La Crone
xxxxxxxxxxxxxxxxxxxx
Burlingame CA 94010

The Honorable Carl Levin
And Panel Members of the Senate
Permanent Subcommittee on Investigations,
United States Senate
269 Russell Senate Office Building
Washington, D.C. 20510-2202

Dear Senator Levin:

Enclosed five copies of my book titled The Depression of 2008: They Did It to Us Again for you and selected members of your committee. Also included are copies of pages detailing the gift stock compensation of three Goldman Sachs CEOs. The book provides a definitive explanation of how management insiders are skimming shareholders' money.

I explain in the book the reason behind why executive insiders make loans that will default. Executives are driven by sales of these loans to increase corporate earnings. Corporate earnings translate into a higher stock price, and a higher stock price translates into maximization of executive gift stock compensation. The book goes a step further and explains that gift stock compensation is a form of equity skimming that amounts to a Ponzi scheme. Executive stock compensation leads to greedy wealth transfers from widows and orphans that meet the criteria of fraud on the market. No rational person would expose their life's savings to certain loss from such a scam. Just three of Goldman Sachs executives have taken over a billion dollars in shareholders' money through gift stocks. The only way that money taken out by these executive insiders will be replaced is through new investors. I have included five pages of detail showing the total gift and awarded stock compensation in dollars for Henry Paulson ($508,405,777.60), John Thain ($426,406,201.40, and Lloyd Blankfein ($321,833,104.19). Just these three CEOs have drained from stockholders' equity accounts $1,256,645,083.19. Executive insiders are using gift stocks in a self dealing scheme to compete with investors for investors' money, and investors are losing. I have a data set showing twenty-five executives from just five companies received over 102 million gift shares. This means that 102 million people who bought a share of stock in one of these companies have or will be cashed out by executive insiders. Shareholders who have lost their life savings in stock investment equity were not sophisticated investors, but widows and orphans.

Please accept the book and supporting detail as evidence in support of Goldman Sachs charges of fraud.

Sincere regards,

Dr. Michael La Crone, MBA, DBA (Finance)